A Crabtree Roots Book
Un libro de Las Raíces de Crabtree

FARM ANIMAL FRIENDS
Animales de granja amistosos

COWS
VACAS

AMY CULLIFORD
SANTIAGO OCHOA

Crabtree Publishing
crabtreebooks.com

School-to-Home Support for Caregivers and Teachers

This book helps children grow by letting them practice reading. Here are a few guiding questions to help the reader with building his or her comprehension skills. Possible answers appear here in red.

Before Reading:

- What do I think this book is about?
    - *This book is about cows.*
    - *This book is about cows that live on farms.*

- What do I want to learn about this topic?
    - *I want to learn about all kinds of cows.*
    - *I want to learn what colors a cow can be.*

During Reading:

- I wonder why...
    - *I wonder why cows have spots.*
    - *I wonder why cows say moo.*

- What have I learned so far?
    - *I have learned that cows can be different colors.*
    - *I have learned that some cows can make milk.*

After Reading:

- What details did I learn about this topic?
    - *I have learned that cows can be brown.*
    - *I have learned that not all cows make milk.*

- Read the book again and look for the vocabulary words.
    - *I see the word **farm** on page 5 and the word **milk** on page 10. The other vocabulary words are found on page 14.*

This is a **cow**.

Esta es una **vaca**.

These cows are on a **farm**.

Estas vacas están en una **granja**.

Some cows are brown.

Algunas vacas son cafés.

4847

Some cows are black and white.

Algunas vacas son negras y blancas.

Some cows make **milk**.

Algunas vacas producen **leche**.

All cows can moo!

¡Todas las vacas
pueden mugir!

Words to Know
Palabras para aprender

cow
vaca

farm
granja

milk
leche

28 Words

This is a **cow**.

These cows are on a **farm**.

Some cows are brown.

Some cows are black and white.

Some cows make **milk**.

All cows can moo!

29 palabras

Esta es una **vaca**.

Estas vacas están en una **granja**.

Algunas vacas son cafés.

Algunas vacas son blancas y negras.

Algunas vacas producen **leche**.

¡Todas las vacas pueden mugir!

FARM ANIMAL FRIENDS
Animales de granja amistosos

COWS
VACAS

Crabtree Publishing

crabtreebooks.com 800-387-7650

Written by: Amy Culliford
Translation by: Santiago Ochoa
Designed by: Rhea Wallace
Series Development: James Earley
Proofreader: Kathy Middleton
Educational Consultant: Christina Lemke M.Ed.
Photographs: Shutterstock: Clara Bastian: cover (tl); Sebastian Knight: cover (tr); Oligo22: cover (b); Anton Havelaar: p. 1; Clara Bastian: p. 3, 12, 14; Maxy Me: p. 4, 14; L.M. Dunn: p. 7; SGr: p. 8-9; RedTC: p. 11, 14

Published in Canada
Crabtree Publishing
616 Welland Ave.
St. Catharines, Ontario
L2M 5V6

Published in the United States
Crabtree Publishing
347 Fifth Avenue,
Suite 1402-145
New York, NY, 10016

Library and Archives Canada Cataloguing in Publication
Available at the Library and Archives Canada

Library of Congress Cataloging-in-Publication Data
Available at the Library of Congress

Paperback: 9781039624443
Ebook: 9781039625280
Epub: 9781039624863

Printed in the U.S.A./CP202510